Why Children are Welcome to the Lord's Supper

Some Questions & Answers About

Paedocommunion

Jeffrey J. Meyers

Why Children are Welcome to the Lord's Supper
Some Questions & Answers About Paedocommunion
By Jeffrey J. Meyers

Copyright © 2024 Jeffrey J. Meyers
Athanasius Press
715 Cypress Street
West Monroe, Louisiana, 71291
www.athanasiuspress.org

Cover design and typesetting: Rachel Rosales

ISBN: 978-1-957726-18-2

Printed in the United States of America.

Quick Reference

"Let the little children come to me and do not hinder them, for to such belongs the kingdom of heaven."
—Matthew 19:14

Introduction & Overview

Whether baptized children are invited to the Lord's Table is not simply a technical or procedural question about church government or tradition, but has significant implications for how we understand baptism, the composition of the church, the function of the Lord's Supper in the liturgy and for Christian living, the discipleship of little children, our alignment with our Lord's attitude towards children, and more.

When we baptize an infant do we think that the rite merely pictures something that hopefully will happen later in the child's life? Or does God at the font formally and publicly covenant with the child such that she is *united* to the body of Christ? And if baptized children are *members* of the body of Christ, shouldn't they be invited to eat of the "one loaf" of the Lord's Supper? Is there a place at the Table for our very young members of the body of Christ? Or should the Supper be reduced to a *devotional aid* for mature Christian adults who can utilize the symbols of bread and wine to contemplate inwardly the meaning of the ritual? Is the church *divided* between those whom God feeds at the Table and little children who must wait until they can maturely articulate their faith publicly before they can eat with Jesus with the rest of the church family?

These and many other weighty questions about the Gospel, the Church, worship, Protestant tradition, and the sacraments are closely related to the question of paedocommunion. There's no way to answer all these questions in this booklet. I have included a short list of recommended reading at the end to help those who want to pursue these issues in more detail. But the only way to begin to address adequately those substantial concerns is to examine Scripture first to determine the status of covenanted children with reference to the Communion Table. I will work through the biblical evidence, starting with the Hebrew Scriptures, then answer a few questions about church history and tradition. I will conclude by answering a few practical questions about the meaning and practice of paedocommunion.

Question 1: Can you give some bullet points that will summarize what you will argue in more detail in this booklet?

- Because baptized children are members of the body of Christ, they are welcome to eat and drink at the Lord's Supper.

- Children were considered full members of Israel and partook of the sacramental meals in the Hebrew Scriptures, including the Passover.

- The Jewish practice of bar mitzvah was a post-New Testament innovation. And even today bar- and bat-mitzvah are not required for children to eat the Passover meal with the Jewish family.

- Moses insisted that Israel's little ones be released from Egypt with the adults to join them for the Feast (Exod. 10:9-10). All the adults and children were baptized in the Red Sea and ate and drank together in the wilderness (1. Cor. 10:1-5).

- Baptized children are members of the body of Christ and therefore have a right to eat with the rest of the church family at the Lord's Table, even if some consider them to be weaker, less honorable, or unpresentable (1 Cor. 12:21-27). Baptism qualifies one to eat at the Table, not theological or intellectual acumen.

- As members of the body of Christ, baptized children are part of the "one loaf" and should be partakers of the bread at the Table with the adults (1 Cor. 10:17). The one loaf symbolizes the entire body of Christ.

- In 1 Corinthians 11 Paul corrects the divisive *behavior* of the *adults* and calls on them to "discern/judge the body," which is a reference to the unity of the *local body* of Christ and not about where the ascended, human *body* of Jesus is in relationship to the bread. The "examining" and "discerning" have to do with how the *adult* members of the church are treating other members, especially at the Table. Paul's conclusion is for them to "wait for" or "share with one another" (11:33).

- Ironically, excluding children from the Table is a form of failing to "discern/judge the body," and in an overweening attempt to be faithful to this admonition those who exclude children are inadvertently violating the very command they are seeking to honor.

- Baptized children were invited to the Table until the doctrine of transubstantiation took hold in the Western church (around A.D. 1000; the Eastern church has always practiced paedocommunion, and still does). The Eucharistic bread and wine became too scary for children to handle. Eventually, the wine was also withheld from the laity over fears of spillage.

- Some fifteenth- and sixteenth-century Reformers sought to restore baptized children to the Supper (Jan Hus and Wolfgang Musculus, for example), but unfortunately the Reformation didn't carefully address this issue, and doctrinal precision and intellectual understanding overshadowed everything.

- Children learn that they belong to and are loved by Jesus when they are welcome to the Table with the rest of the body of Christ. They may not *understand* the sermon, and they may not comprehend what is going on in the Supper (who really can?), but they can *experience* exclusion or inclusion when the Supper is served.

- In our homes we don't wait for our children to be able to articulate what it means to belong to the family before they can eat. They learn the meaning and significance of the family meal while eating at the table. This is how it should be at the church's family meal as well.

- Maturity is needed for *ruling* and *voting*, not for *eating*; for making complicated decisions, not for feeding on Jesus. Jesus feeds every baptized Christian at his Table, but not everyone is qualified to make judgments that bear upon the doctrine and government of his church. We distinguish between communing and voting members.

Questions Relating to Israel & the Hebrew Scriptures

Moses said, "We will go with our young and our old. We will go with our sons and daughters and with our flocks and herds, for we must hold a feast to Yahweh." But Pharaoh said to them, "Yahweh be with you, if ever I let you and your little ones go!" —Exodus 10:9-10

Question 2: Did young children partake of the sacramental meals in Israel?

Yes. The basic argument from the Hebrew Scriptures is straightforward. It assumes two standard Reformed biblical-theological presuppositions:

1. The essential unity of the Old and New Covenant with respect to *salvation* and *sanctification*

(Gen. 15:6; Rom. 4:13; Rom. 2:25-29; Gal. 3:6-18; Westminster Confession of Faith 7:5, 6).

2. The essential unity of the Old and New Covenant with respect to the *sacraments* (1 Cor. 10:1-5; Col. 2:11, 12). According to the Westminster Confession of Faith 7:5, "the sacraments of the Old Testament, in regard to the spiritual things thereby signified and exhibited, were, for substance, the same with those of the New."

Therefore, if we can establish that the covenant children in the Old Covenant participated in the sacramental communion meals, we create a strong case for the continuity of that practice in the New Testament, unless we have explicit evidence to the contrary.

One of the highlights of most of Israel's feasts and sacrificial rituals was the covenantal meal shared by the whole community. The primary food for these covenantal meals—the meat—was taken from the fellowship (or "peace") offerings sacrificially slain and offered on the altar by the priests. After the peace offering had been made, the priests took the cooked meat and gave it back to the worshiper to eat with his family or in the case of a major feast, he distributed it to the people gathered for the feast.

> You shall build an altar to Yahweh your God of uncut stones. And you shall offer burnt offerings on it to Yahweh your God, and you shall sacrifice peace offerings and shall eat there, and you shall rejoice before Yahweh your God (Deut. 27:6-7).

In Israel small children participated with the household in these sacramental meals. If the child was eating solid food, he participated in the sacrificial feast. The nourishing sacraments of the Old Covenant were many and varied, but they are all fulfilled in the Lord's Supper. The basic argument, again, is: If all the covenantal meals of the Old Covenant are fulfilled in the one covenantal meal of the New Covenant—the Lord's Supper—and if children partook in the Old Covenant communion meals, therefore, unless there is some explicit New Testament statement to the contrary, children in the New Covenant ought also to eat with the rest of the Lord's people at the New Covenant communal feast.

First, consider the sacrificial-covenantal meals that the entire *household* ate when the family offered a fellowship (or "peace") offering (Lev. 3). Deuteronomy 12:7 states that when the one place of worship is established (Jerusalem, as we later discover) "there you shall eat before the Lord your God, and you shall rejoice in all to which you have put your hand, you and your households, in which the Lord your God has blessed you" (see also Deut. 27:6-7, quoted above). Clearly, "households" refer to all the members of the family: adults, children, and in the Hebrew Scriptures, servants as well. It is simply incredible to believe that when a family made that rare trip up to Jerusalem to offer a fellowship offering and to eat a rich covenantal meal in God's presence (Israelites did not usually eat this well) that only the mature adults would be able to participate in the dinner. It is hardly conceivable that the children would not have been able to eat with the rest of the family.

Where is the evidence that they were excluded from the Old Covenant sacramental meals? The *burden of proof* lies with those who think that children were excluded from these meals. Where is the Old Testament command or the illustration that indicates that children were barred from these Communion meals? If you think the Passover regulations provide reasons that bar young children from eating, you have been misinformed about the meaning of those passages in Exodus 12. We will deal with the Passover rules shortly.

Second, biblical evidence for child communion can be found in the presence of small children at the major feasts of Israel—feasts where the Israelites ate sacrificial covenant meals with their families and each other. The worship services of the church are not for "adults only," but must have included infants and small children. The Old Covenant worship gatherings included children. God commanded them to bring their little ones! When Joshua recited the whole of the Law of Moses to the people, "the entire congregation, with the women, the little ones, and the strangers" gathered and stood to hear the Word of God (Josh. 8:35). These kinds of covenantal gatherings occurred throughout the history of Israel, and even though children are not always explicitly mentioned, nevertheless, they are often present at these feasts (2 Chron. 20:13; Ezra 8:21; Joel 2:15-16). There is certainly no good reason to believe that they were not present.

Third, 1 Samuel 1:1-8 provides us with a specific instance of a family—a man, his wife, and his children—partaking of the sacramental food of a peace offering at one of the major feasts of Israel. Here Elkanah, as the godly covenantal head of his family, takes his entire family up for the yearly feasts and sacrifices (Deut. 16:6). The feast could very well have been the Passover. According to verse 4, "Whenever the time came for Elkanah to make an offering, he would give portions to Peninah his wife and to all her sons and daughters." Note the word "all." No ages are given. All the sons and daughters partook. The normal practice would be for the whole family to participate in these sacrificial sacraments. Remember, the food taken from the sacrificial altar and eaten by the worshipers in the Old Covenant is equivalent to the food taken from the final sacrifice and distributed to the New Covenant people of God. The Westminster Confession of Faith 27.5 reminds us that "the sacraments of the Old Testament, in regard to spiritual things thereby signified and exhibited, were, for substance, the same with those of the New."

Men, women, and children, according to Nehemiah 12:43, participated in a great sacrificial feast convoked to celebrate the dedication and purification of the new walls of Jerusalem: "Also that day they offered great sacrifices and rejoiced, for God had made them rejoice with great joy; the wives also and the children, so that the joy of Jerusalem was heard afar off." The great sacrifices refer to the large number of animals killed and cooked; the rejoicing of the people would have consisted primarily in eating such a sumptuous meal while praising God for his gracious provisions. Would the children have had to eat something else? Would they have been purposefully excluded from these covenant meals because they were not old enough? Do we find any evidence that this ever happened?

Fourth, an argument from the Hebrew Scriptures for young child Communion arises out of a thoughtful consideration of 1 Corinthians 10:1-5. Consider the manna that Israel ate in the wilderness.

> I want you to know, brethren, that our fathers were all under the cloud, and all passed through the sea, and all were baptized into Moses in the cloud and in the sea, and all ate the same supernatural food and all drank the same supernatural drink. For they drank from the supernatural Rock which followed them, and the Rock was Christ.

Here Paul reminds the Corinthian church that Old Covenant Israel experienced the sacraments typologically, and that this means we can learn something from these Old Covenant stories about the New Covenant church, and specifically, how we are to behave with reference to the New Covenant sacraments. Paul refers to the crossing of the Red Sea as Israel's *baptism* and their eating the manna in the wilderness as their *communion* meal with Christ, thereby drawing a direct parallel between the spiritual food (food in which the Holy Spirit is present to give life to those who eat) of the old Covenant (manna and water) and the Spiritual food of the New Covenant (bread and wine). "All were baptized into Moses in the cloud and in the sea," Paul explains, "all ate the same spiritual food, and all drank the same spiritual drink" (1 Cor. 10:2-3). Jesus makes this point also in John 6:31-65. Now, the question is this: who partook of these Old Covenant communion meals? The answer is that "all" did, adults and children. What else was there to eat in the wilderness but the manna and water that God provided? The burden of proof lies on the one who would deny that children ate these covenantal meals.

Question 3: But what about the Passover meal? I thought children had to wait to eat that.

Some think that the Passover meal, a particularly solemn example of a fellowship (peace) offering, provides proof that little children did *not* eat at these sacrificial meals. The regulations and explanation of the Passover meal, however, offer no positive proof for this. In fact, the Passover meal will provide us with a *fifth* argument from the Hebrew Scriptures for admitting young children to the Communion Table. The controversy centers on Exodus 12:26:

> And it shall be when your children say to you, "What do you mean by this service?" that you shall say, "It is the Passover sacrifice of the Lord, who passed over the houses of the children of Israel in Egypt when He struck the Egyptians and delivered our households."

This passage does not establish that such "question asking" by the child was the *prerequisite* for *participating* in the meal. The very idea that the child must first ask this question *before* he is allowed to eat must be *read into* the passage. Neither does this passage mandate some kind of ceremony before which the child would not be allowed to share in the sacrificial meal. Nor is there any evidence that ancient Israel practiced such a ceremony as the Jews today call *bar mitzvah*. The *bar mitzvah* rituals have no bearing whatsoever on the question of young child Communion. And the *bar mitzvah* is not what qualifies a young Jewish child to eat the Passover with the family; rather, is a rite of passage signaling the child's assumption of his mature responsibility within the community. We will return to the *bar mitzvah* argument shortly.

Consider Exodus 12:23-27.

> For Yahweh will pass through to slay the Egyptians; and when he sees the blood on the lintel and on the two doorposts, Yahweh will pass over the door, and will not allow the destroyer to enter your houses to slay you. You shall observe this rite as an ordinance for you and for your sons forever. And when you come to the land which Yahweh will give you, as he has promised, you shall keep this service.
>
> And when your children say to you, "What do you mean by this service?" you shall say, "It is the sacrifice of Yahweh's Passover, for he passed over the houses of the people of Israel in Egypt, when he slew the Egyptians but spared our houses."

The most natural way to understand those final two verses (Exodus 12:26-27) is that when the children ask the parents why *the family is eating* such an extraordinary meal, the parents would then explain the significance to them *in the context of the dinner*.

Exodus 12:3 confirms this. Here we read that "every man shall take for himself a lamb, according to the house of their fathers, a lamb for a family." Exodus 12:4 requires that every man, acting as the covenantal head of the family, estimate the size of his family (including wife, children, and servants, etc.) to determine the appropriate size of the dinner lamb. He is to take a lamb "according to the number of persons/souls" in his household. This was a family meal. As if to emphasize this, God commands in Deuteronomy 12:7 that "the households" shall celebrate by eating together the sacrificial meals. The entire family or household was to eat the roasted lamb together.

Further evidence that children were not excluded from the Passover meal can be found in Exodus 12:43-49. Here God specifically lists those who would *not* be allowed to participate in the Passover. The distinguishing characteristic, which forbade participation, was *not being circumcised*. Circumcision was a sign of being in covenant with God; it was the sign of the righteousness that Israel possessed by faith (Rom. 4:11). The small children of Israel were in covenant with God. They had the right to enjoy the salvation and fellowship of their Savior and Covenant Lord. To imagine that the youngest in the family ate something else or just watched while the adult men ate the Passover is ludicrous considering the familial, covenantal assumptions of the Hebrew Scriptures. For example, one recent book on the Lord's Supper argues that neither women nor children partook of the Passover, but *merely watched* the adult men eat! That's unbelievable.

Remember, 1 Sam. 1:1-8, where Elkanah travels yearly to Shiloh for the annual festivals. He takes his family and the entire family partakes of the sacrificial food (1 Samuel 1:4). This was most likely a Passover meal. The entire family rejoiced together in their covenant meal with the Lord (Deut. 12:7).

The Passover is one of the primary typological forerunners to the sacrament of the Lord's Supper; and *there is no evidence in the Hebrew Scriptures that children were excluded from the Passover meal.* After all, what else was there to eat? To even suggest that the children sat there and watched as the parents ate strikes at the heart of God's covenantal familial relations with his people. This same separation is present today in many congregations. Adults eat dinner with Jesus and the children watch. The adults and parents of the congregation are again assured of their place in the family of God during the Communion meal, but the children are excluded. Think of it this way. Do you put the children out on the porch or in the basement when the adults eat the family meal? Will you separate them until they can articulate the meaning of the meal?

Finally, remembering that Jesus lived during the Old Covenant era, there are all those passages in the New Testament where Jesus invites the little children to come to him, even to be carried to him. Jesus also warns the disciples of the terrible curse on those who "hinder" or "do not permit" little children to come to him (see Matt. 18:1-6; 19:13-15; Mark 9:33-37; 10:13-16; Luke 9:46-48; 18:15-16).

How strange it would be if we would gather around the family table to eat and yet exclude our young children from eating dinner! If the Lord's dinner Table serves the family of God, why then are the little ones not also served? Are they not to be fed at God's family dinner table? Does Jesus only want to feed and nourish the adults? If at the Communion Table we are all eating dinner with Jesus, shouldn't we let the little children come to him?

The evidence presented here has been suggestive rather than exhaustive. Nevertheless, we can be assured that the Old Testament presupposes the presence of children at the communion meals. To suggest otherwise places the burden of proof on those who would keep children from the Table.

If we could be careful not to let our *traditions* obscure the evidence, the biblical facts are obvious. The Israelites' "little ones" were delivered from Egypt, were "baptized" in the Red Sea, included in the covenant God made with Israel on Mt. Sinai, and participated in all the benefits and responsibilities of the covenant (circumcision, Passover, water from the rock, manna, the sacrifices, etc.). They participated in the sacraments of nourishment and communion (Exod. 12:3; 1 Sam. 1:1-8; 2 Chron. 20:13; 1 Cor. 10:1-4). There is nothing to suggest that they were excluded until they reached a certain age or attained a specific level of knowledge.

Question 4: I've always been taught that since the Lord's Supper is a continuation of the Passover, we should follow the same admission procedures as the Jews. Their children have to wait until they go through bar-mitzvah at age thirteen before they can eat the Passover meal. Shouldn't we follow the same procedure?

The fiction that children did not eat the Passover meal until they were thirteen is widespread in Protestant churches. First of all, just because the Jews today practice a rite of passage ritual like *bar mitzvah* does not mean that the Old Testament Jews had any such practice. There is no evidence that the Old Testament Israelites practiced *bar mitzvah*. And understand that for modern Jews the *bar mitzvah* ritual is not about admitting children to the Passover meal. They have already been eating with everyone years before they go through *bar mitzvah*.

The idea that an Old Covenant child was not allowed to eat the Passover until he was thirteen is impossible to support from the Bible. Briefly, again, for the sake of clarity, I want to be certain the reader understands the force of the argument. The ceremony of *bar mitzvah* developed sometime *after* the first century A.D. and was codified in the Talmud.

The argument against infant and young child Communion is most often stated with reference to the Passover. The argument can be summed up as follows: Since the Lord's Supper is the New Covenant equivalent of the Old Covenant Passover, and since we know from Exodus 12:26 that children who did not have the intellectual capacity to ask questions about the meaning of the festival could not partake, therefore, children who are not yet old enough to ask the Exodus 12:26 question about the New Covenant Supper are not yet qualified to partake of the Lord's Supper.

There are three problems with this line of reasoning.

First, even if we grant the cogency of this argument, it cannot exclude all but the very youngest of children. The ages of the children asking the questions are not mentioned in the text of Exodus 12. Neither is there really any clue in the text itself that question-asking is the prerequisite for eating. But for the sake of the argument, let's grant that the child must be able to ask this kind of question before he can eat. So if we grant that question-asking is the necessary precondition for eating, how does this exclude young children from the Passover? At the most it would exclude very young children who are not able to ask questions. So, assuming that this question-asking is the biblical criteria for admittance to the Lord's Table, then the church ought to admit many young children, much younger than those we presently admit. *How does Exodus 12:26 rule out younger children?* I know my kids began to ask these kinds of questions when they were very young. In fact, that's all three-year-olds do—ask questions!

But someone will say, "Yes, that's all well and fine, but we know that children in the Old Covenant were not admitted to the Passover feast until they were thirteen years old." Do we? No, we do not. This developed as a post-Christian Jewish practice. This is exactly the issue we are trying to analyze. There is no biblical or historical evidence to suggest that only those older than thirteen ate the Passover meal. In fact, even if we granted that this "question asking" was used as a criterion for admittance to Table, nevertheless, if we just to stick to the biblical text, little children who ask questions about the Passover, whether three or thirteen ought be admitted. There is no age limit set in the text. And if there is not one, it is not because the Bible is hesitant to assign age specifications. It does so in many other places in the Hebrew Scriptures. Even if for the sake of the argument we concede that question-asking was required before eating the Passover, I conclude that my two-year-old who asks question about Communion is qualified to come to the Table and eat dinner with Jesus.

Second, there is a serious question about the *propriety* of seeing Exodus 12:26 as a criterion for participation in the meal. The text itself does not actually address the question of child participation in the Passover. Why must we assume that the child who asks this question is not yet a partaker of the meal? The text itself nowhere hints at this. It would be more natural to assume that the child was eating the meal with the family when the question is asked. Why must we assume that the child who asks this question is thereby *qualified* for participation? There is no stipulation in the text itself that requires the child to ask the question *before* he may eat. Is there anything in the text itself that indicates that children partake *after* they ask this question?

No. Nothing at all. One must read this idea into the text. Surely it is much more likely that the whole family eats the meal (everyone who is old enough to eat solid food), and that it is within the context of this family meal that the children ask these questions? Over time, as they mature, the children would learn more and more of God's saving love for *them* and of their responsibility to their Savior God. After all, the children were also delivered from Egypt with the adults. Surely this is the natural and best way to interpret what's going on at the family Passover meal.

Someone may question this line of reasoning, saying that we shouldn't *assume* that the children ate. All of this assuming will get us into trouble. Using our argument against us, someone may suggest that we are also making unwarranted assumptions that have no basis in the text itself. Because the text doesn't explicitly state that children ate the meal, we should not assume it. Wouldn't it be safer to stick to the text itself and not make unwarranted assumptions?

Well, yes, it would be better to stick to the text. What does the text say? It says that the whole family ate. Now, it is true, children are not explicitly identified as actually eating. Are they not part of the family? Is it really *unwarranted* to assume that they ate with the rest of the family? Isn't it absurd to believe that the entire family ate *except* the children—they watched as the adults ate! When we read that the father chose and prepared a lamb for the whole family (Exod. 12:4), we have every reason to believe that the wife and children and any members of the extended family ate the Passover meal together. When we read that the father was to choose a lamb "according to the number of souls" in his household, are we forcing an alien logic on the text when we say that the children were to be included among the "souls" belonging to the family? Besides, Presbyterian and Reformed theologians have used this form of argument to defend infant baptism in the New Testament. We argue that the practice of household baptism in the New Testament surely must have included infants.

Not to believe that the "family" includes children leads to silly and absurd conclusions. Read through the passage (Exod. 12) and see if it anywhere makes reference to *women* partaking of the Passover meal? It doesn't. Therefore, is it safe to assume that women didn't partake either? After all, the text does not say so explicitly! Let's not make unwarranted assumptions. Are we to believe that the women and children sat at the table while the father and all the circumcised adult males ate? When it says "a lamb for the family" does this really mean "a lamb for the adult men"?

All this discussion about *assumptions* is not helpful. We don't really need to *assume* anything. Exodus 12:4 commands the father to get a lamb large enough for the whole family, to get one "according to the number of souls" in the family. The entire context of Exodus 12 teaches that this is a family meal. Exodus 12:43-49 carefully lists those who would be forbidden from participating. The biblical evidence is that the entire family ate at the feasts (again, see Deut. 12:7). Elkanah gives portions of the sacrificial food to "his wife and to all her sons and daughters" (I Sam. 1:4). Everybody passed through the Red Sea and ate of the manna in the wilderness, men, women and children (Exod. 10:24; I Cor. 10:1ff). When we arrive at such outlandish conclusions such as the one we have been critiquing, namely, that women and children did not eat with the family during covenantal festival meals, we are guilty of reading our own modern presuppositions back into the text.

The erroneous argument that we have been dealing with above—children did not eat the Passover meal—*used* to be the favorite argument of those who opposed young child Communion. Now, wisely, most scholarly opponents have dropped that argument. It still floats around in popular circles, but it is impossible to maintain in light of the Biblical data.

Third, the problem with the argument that only thirteen-year-old children and older ate the Passover meal is that it assumes the New Covenant sacrament is *merely* an extension of the Passover; or I should say it supposes that the Lord's Supper is *only* an extension of the Passover. The Passover indeed became the preeminent fellowship offering and sacrificial meal in the Old Covenant, but it's not the only one. All the sacrificial meals of the Old Covenant typologically prefigure the New Covenant Communion meal (I Cor. 10:1ff). To isolate the Passover without looking at the other covenant meals is too reductionistic. Remember, the Lord's Supper is not merely an extension of the Passover. It is the fulfillment of all the covenantal/fellowship meals of the Hebrew Scriptures. Even the best of those who argue against paedocommunion acknowledge this much. Peter Leithart's comments make a fitting conclusion to our discussion of the evidence for young child Communion from the Hebrew Scriptures:

> *Whenever the lay Israelites were allowed to eat a sacrificial/sacramental meal, their children were invited too.* This was true of the Passover (Exod. 12:3-4), the peace offering (Lev. 7:15-21), the other annual feasts of Israel (Deut. 14:22-29; 16:9-14), and the wilderness meals

(1 Cor. 10:1-4)... There is not a single example of a common meal that excluded children."

Questions Relating to Jesus & the New Testament

And they were bringing children to him that he might touch them, and the disciples rebuked them. But when Jesus saw it, he was outraged and said to them, "Let the children come to me; do not hinder them, for to such belongs the kingdom of God. —Mark 10:13-14

Question 5: What would Jesus say about young child Communion? Is this issue really all that important to him? Is it wise and beneficial to the church to introduce another controversy? Why can't we Presbyterians just continue with the way we have done it for hundreds of years?

Perhaps the first thing to say is that controversy is often God's way of advancing his church. Dispute brings the truth to light and forces us to come to grips with portions of his Word that may have lain buried under a pile of erroneous presuppositions. Second, this controversy is not insignificant, but has far reaching implications for church life, family life, and it even has broader cultural applications as well. I confess that my gut feeling on this subject, especially considering the current practice of most Evangelical and Reformed churches, can be described as nothing short of terror. I do not say this to be overly sensational. The words of Jesus give rise to my strong feelings, and I hope that after you come to grips with Jesus' concern for covenant children you will feel the same way. Earlier I discussed our Reformed confessional standards and the Old Testament. Now we will examine Jesus' care and concern for covenant children.

Matthew records an incident in Jesus' ministry when "little children were brought to Him that He might lay hands on them and pray, but the disciples rebuked them" (Matt. 19:13-14). We are not told why the apostles rebuked those bringing the children, but maybe that's because their evil and foolish motives are so transparent. It is the fact that they hindered/obstructed the children that so infuriated Jesus. No doubt they thought that Jesus had better things to do than to waste time with little children. After all, he has *adults* to teach and disciple. Let's get serious, the disciples must have thought, we have more important business to attend to. If news of this gets around, and parents think that Jesus will do this kind of thing for every child, then we'll be bogged down with all these kids. Please notice that Jesus simply ignored the disciples and received the children into his presence. Then he roundly rebuked his disciples for their ignorance.

Mark's account (10:13-16) of the same or a similar incident more fully reveals Jesus' attitude toward the disciples who rebuked those who carried the children to Jesus. Jesus was *indignant* ("very angry," "greatly displeased," even "boiling mad") when he rebuked the disciples: "Permit the little children to come to me, and do not hinder them; for of such is the kingdom of God." Jesus sternly warns the disciples (and us) not to hinder (or forbid) little children to come to him. The reason: *children like these belong to the kingdom of God.* In this context, Jesus' statement does *not* mean—nor can it possibly be grammatically construed to mean—that those who are members of the kingdom are *like* little children. Jesus is not here making an analogy or using a simile to help the disciples understand how an adult enters the kingdom. Jesus does make an analogy between children and entrance into the kingdom in the verse proceeding after this one. But here in verse 14 he means that *the subjects and members of the kingdom are children* like these covenant children that have been brought to me. These children belong to the kingdom of God, Jesus tells his disciples; and there are other children such as these who also belong to the kingdom of God. You better be careful how you treat them!

When we properly understand the second clause upon which Jesus based his rebuke ("for of such are the kingdom of God"), then we can properly appreciate the nature of the rebuke. It is as if Jesus had said: "Do you think that my kingdom is for adults only? Is the king too busy to be bothered by children? Are they to be barred from my presence because you think they don't have the necessary maturity or intellectual capabilities? Will they contaminate me because they are immature and childish? Observe how significant these children are to me. They are as close to me as you disciples are, and I bless them in the same way I bless you. Learn a lesson from this, men. Be careful not to excommunicate from my presence these little children. I desire to commune with them!"

John Murray sums up Jesus' intent with a very telling paragraph:

> We must conclude, therefore, that when Jesus says, "Of such is the kingdom of God," he is not speaking of the class resembling little children but is referring to little children them-

selves and affirms unmistakably that little children are members of the kingdom of God. *The
thought expressed is not the quality which fits
a person for entrance into the kingdom of God
but rather the place which little children themselves are to have in the redemptive ministry of
Jesus and their relation to the kingdom of God*
(John Murray, *Christian Baptism*, 62-63, emphasis mine).

John Calvin's comments on Matthew 19:14, "Suffer the little children to come to me and do not forbid
them," are helpful. This passage is worth quoting in
full. Please read it carefully.

Jesus declares that he wishes to receive children; and at length, taking them in his arms,
he not only embraces, but blesses them by the
laying on of hands; from which *we infer that
his grace is extended even to those who are of that
age.* And no wonder; for sin the whole race of
Adam is shut up under the sentence of death,
all from the least to the greatest must perish,
except those who are rescued only by the Re-
deemer. To exclude from the grace of redemp-
tion those who are of that age would be too
cruel; and therefore, it is not without reason

that we employ this passage as a shield against the Anabaptists [Baptists]. They refuse baptism to infants, because infants are incapable of understanding that mystery which is denoted by it. We, on the other hand, maintain that, since baptism is the pledge and figure of the forgiveness of sins, and likewise of adoption by God, it ought not to be denied to infants, whom God adopts and washes with the blood of his Son. Their objection, that repentance and newness of life are also denoted by it, is easily answered. *Infants are renewed by the Spirit of God, according to the capacity of their age, till that power, which was concealed within them, grows by degrees, and becomes fully manifest at the proper time.* Again, when they argue that there is no other way in which we are reconciled to God, and become heirs of adoption, than by faith, we admit this to adults, but, with respect to infants, this passage demonstrates it to be false. Certainly, the laying on of hands was not a trifling or empty sign, and the prayers of Christ were not idly wasted in air. But he could not present the infants solemnly to God without giving them purity. And for what did he pray for them, but that they might be received into the number of the children of God? *Hence it follows, that they were renewed by the Spirit to the hope of salvation.* In short, by embracing them, he testified that they were reckoned by Christ among his flock. And if they were partakers of the spiritual gifts, which are represented by Baptism, it is unreasonable that they should be deprived of the outward sign. But it is presumption and sacrilege to drive far from the fold of Christ those whom he cherishes in his bosom, and to shut the door, and exclude as strangers those whom he does not wish to be forbidden to him (Calvin's comments on Matt. 19:14; emphasis mine).

True, Calvin uses this passage to argue for infant baptism, but he just as easily and without contradiction could have also used it to argue for infant Communion. If children are "brought to Jesus" in the sacrament of baptism, they no less come to Jesus in the sacrament of Communion. If children are properly subjects of the kingdom, and if the sacrament of the kingdom is the Lord's Supper—to which we are invited as subjects to the royal feast—and if the living presence of the Lord Jesus is symbolized and experienced in a special way at the Communion Table, then why are children excluded? Why are they hindered from coming to Jesus and eating with him? Why are they not "permitted" to approach the covenant family Table to receive the assurance of Jesus' love and his promise of nourishment? Why are they not allowed to participate in the "cup of blessing" (1 Cor. 10:16) and so receive Jesus' blessing just as they did in his arms during his physical ministry on earth? Why could little children come to Jesus when he was *physically* present during his earthly ministry and yet now must be barred from his *sacramental* presence in the Lord's Supper? How else can children come to Jesus today? Who needs the reassurance of Christ's sacramental presence in the bread and wine more than little children? They may sing "Jesus loves me," but they ought also to be assured of his love when they come to him for food and drink at his Table.

Jesus goes on to draw an analogy between children and adults who enter the kingdom of God (Mark 10:15). He says, in effect, don't you know that adult conversion is not the paradigm for entrance into the kingdom? No, precisely the reverse is the case. Children are models when it comes to entering the kingdom. Modern American Christians need to hear this. We have become overly intellectualistic. We are too adult oriented. For example, we think that the baptism of an adult upon their conversion best reveals the meaning of that sacrament, and so we have a hard time understanding the meaning of infant baptism. In fact, the real meaning of baptism is especially revealed in infant baptism. The meaning of the Gospel is more fully revealed in the baptism of an infant. An infant is not self-sufficient. An infant must rely on others in the community of faith to raise him and teach him. An infant does not make the first steps toward God. The infant is passive. God acts on us prior to us acting for or toward him. The sacraments are works of God, *not* works of man. A good Christian is always an infant in his dependence on God. To view Christianity as primarily an adult religion is a modern distortion.

I began this answer with an admission of terror. The reason I am terrified is simple. For close to a millennium now, the Western church has hindered its little ones from coming to Jesus. Communion was withdrawn from little children slowly, here and there, as the doctrine of transubstantiation began to take hold, beginning around A.D. 1000. Before A.D. 1000 the evidence is overwhelming and irrefutable: little children, even infants, communed at the Lord's Table. There is not one shred of positive evidence in the New Testament that *forbids* little children from coming to Jesus' dinner Table with the rest of the family of God, commands and warnings given to disobedient *adults* to examine themselves notwithstanding (1 Cor. 11:28).

Furthermore, there is everything to suggest that covenant children ought to participate in the New Covenant fellowship meal just as they participated in the covenant meals of the Old Covenant, Passover included. I conclude that Jesus is "greatly displeased," even "indignant" about this situation in his church. This is terrifying enough, but there is more.

Consider Matthew 18:1-2. After bringing a child into the midst of his disciples in order to rebuke their sinful preoccupation with who would be the greatest in the kingdom, Jesus solemnly warns them: "And whoever receives one child like this in my name receives me; but whoever causes one of these little ones who believe to stumble, it is better for him that a heavy millstone be hung around his neck, and that he be drowned in the depth of the sea."

A severe curse is pronounced on anyone who would make such a little believer stumble, or as some translations say "scandalize one of these little ones." A *scandalon* is a "stumbling block" put in someone's way so as to cause him to fall. We don't know how old this child was. Matthew called him "a child" (Gr. *paidion*). The Greek word can refer to either an infant or a very young child (Luke 2:21; John 16:21). The word is often used in a pejorative sense to indicate immaturity, childish thinking, etc. (1 Cor. 14:20). This is important.

These "immature, childish" kids are the very children that are called by Jesus "little ones who believe" (Matt. 18:6)! It is not possible to claim that these "little ones who believe" were *mature* children. The very language used to describe them connotes immaturity and childish thinking. Jesus says these little ones are *believers*! These very young children are the ones that we are to take care not to offend or cause to stumble and fall. The consequences of carelessness with regard to this duty are not very pleasant: a millstone hung around the neck before one is thrown into the sea.

This is precisely why we should be fearful. We are culturally and intellectually predisposed against treating young children as Jesus wants them to be treated. In addition, our revivalist tradition in America prejudices us against treating little children as believers because they have not had a certain kind of conversion experience. Moreover, our cerebral Reformed heritage further colors our mindset, and we demand a relatively high level of intellectual capability before these little ones can come to Jesus. In all these ways, no matter what the excuse, we offend little believers whom Jesus desires to come to him.

Moreover, if it is true that the church is the nursery of the kingdom, a microcosmic model for all of civilization—the implications and ramifications of what goes on in the church flow out from the church into all areas of life—then is it any wonder that the twentieth century is so anti-child in its sentiments? As it goes in the church, so it goes in the world. We are the salt of the earth. The city set on a hill sets the example for the world. Could it be that the church in the West has failed to set the example for the world in how we treat children? Is the following analysis all that far fetched:

> In this way [barring young children from Communion], the Church in the West ceased offering the protection of Christ to the children of the West. The results have been slow in coming but are now devastating. Ancient Israel faced the same choice. They were supposed to circumcise their children and bring them to the Passover. When they ignored the festivals (as they almost always did), they fell into child sacrifice, giving their children to Molech. So it was then, so it is today. We now face rampant child pornography, child molestation, child abuse, incest, and abortion. This will not cease until the Church once again welcomes the little children to Jesus. ("Abortion: Its Cause and Cure" by James B. Jordan)

Question 6: What about 1 Corinthians 11:27–30? Are young children able to properly "discern the body"? Can they "examine themselves" sufficiently to approach the Table without bringing judgment upon themselves? How can a very young child examine himself before he comes to the Table, as 1 Corinthians 11 seems to demand?

This question requires some careful analysis. I will answer it in two parts: 1) Can a young child examine himself? 2) Can a young child "discern the body"? These two questions are both related to 1 Corinthians 11:27-30.

First, if anyone would care to argue that a two-year-old cannot self-consciously participate in the Church's Communion meal, then I would argue that logically they must also be denied the family meal at home. When the family gathers for dinner at home, our little ones learn how to behave at the table. Indeed, their understanding of the nature of the family grows and develops as they *experience* the reality of family communion around the table each night. We know that very young children are indeed able to control themselves at the family table, learn when to talk and when to remain silent, discern the appropriate way to participate in the table fellowship, and correct their behavior when they are punished. What is this but "self-examination"? Where in the world did this rationalistic notion that young children do not have the ability to examine themselves come from? The idea is ludicrous. Do Christian parents wait until their children are eight, nine, or thirteen (!) before they begin to teach, train, and punish their children? No. If my three-year-old is acting up at the table, I correct him because I assume that he can discern that there is a right and a wrong way to act at the family table. I assume that he can examine himself, and, truth be told, my assumption is correct.

In the same way, young children are able, *according to their capacity*, to make a confession of their faith ("Jesus loves me"), examine themselves and confess their sins ("I'm sorry, Dad! I won't do it again"), and understand the *rudiments* of what goes on during the celebration of the Lord's supper ("God loves me so much he feeds me, just like Dad and Mom do"). And even though a very young child is still learning to articulate his faith, it does not follow that the child has no faith. Nor does it follow that the child cannot intelligently participate in the meal. A child at his mother's breast may not be able to talk to you about what is going on, but he learns very quickly who his mother is and what she means to him. Therefore, even though the conscious, rational participation of a young child will not normally "measure up" intellectually nor experientially to that of an adult believer, nevertheless, a small child may participate intelligently and self-consciously in the Lord's supper *according to his or her capacity as a child*. A little child will not be able to prepare for Communion *as thoroughly* as an adult, but he or she *can* prepare, and he or she *can* rationally participate, and it is upon this basis, grounded upon their baptism into the church, that young children ought not to be hindered from coming to Jesus at his Table.

At the Lord's Table, children will gradually mature in their understanding that they are sinners, that Jesus loves them, that Jesus died for them, that they must live in obedience to Jesus' commands, and that Jesus feeds them in the Lord's Supper (this list is not meant to be a definitive or exhaustive list)—and all of this happens in the context of their *participation* at the Lord's family Table.

Second, let's dig a little deeper into the issue of self-examination. Traditional Presbyterian theologians regularly cite 1 Corinthians 11:28 as an argument *against* the practice of young child Communion. Children must be able "to examine themselves" before they come to the Table. Supposedly, this text demands a certain level of intellectual capability as well as the capacity to engage in self-conscious introspection, both of which, we are told, small children do not possess. Those who oppose young child Communion never get tired of reminding us that young children simply are not able to fulfill the requirement of "self-examination" required in 1 Corinthians 11.

But, does this text really require the kind of self-examination that Presbyterians have traditionally thought? To whom is the admonition to "examine oneself" directed? Does it truly require an ability to perform internal soul-searching and deep personal introspection to determine whether one is worthy to come to the Table? No, it does not. I believe those who oppose admitting little children to the Lord's Table have overworked this text. In fact, I am convinced that it actually works against the traditional Presbyterian practice of excluding infants from the Table. Traditional Presbyterian theologians need to examine *themselves*. Let me explain.

The verb Paul uses here is *dokimazo*. To bring out the meaning of this Greek word, it may be best to translate 1 Corinthians 11:28 as follows: "Let a man prove himself before he eats..." In this context (1 Cor. 10-12), it refers to the Christian's behavior with respect to the unity of the body of Christ. The whole context of this admonition has to do with behaving in a way that manifests *the unity of the church*. All Christians "participate in the body of Christ. Because there is one loaf, we, who are many, are one body, for we all partake of the one loaf" (1 Cor. 10:16b-17).

The problem in the Corinthian church was that people were behaving at the Supper in a manner that contradicted the reality of the unity of their local church with each other in Christ. They were *divided* at the Table! They were therefore eating unworthily. "Unworthily" (*anaxios*) is an *adverb* that modifies the verb "eat." Paul is not talking about checking to see if you are a worthy *person* before you come to the Table. He is talking about *how* you partake of the Supper. They are eating and drinking in an unworthy manner. He is calling them out for their *behavior* at the Table. Some Corinthian Christians were eating and drinking in an unworthy *manner*, that is, in a way that did not evidence the unity of the body of Christ. The rich Christians were eating with each other and excluding the poorer members of the church. Therefore, "let a man prove himself" refers to their *manner* of participation at the Table, or more broadly, to their relationship with the local body of Christ.

The admonition "Let a man prove himself" means "let a man *show* that he rightly judges the unity of the body of Christ when he comes to the Table. Let his actions *demonstrate* to all that he is one who lives in a manner that manifests his unity with all the brethren, including the poorer members." The evidence of this "self-demonstration" would be the way he treats his brothers in Christ, especially when he partakes of the sacrament—eating in a manner that demonstrates his unity with the body of Christ in the local church. This understanding of the verb "to prove" (*dokimazo*) can be established from the immediate context. Paul says in 1 Corinthians 11:19, "No doubt there have to be divisions among you in order that the proven ones (*oi dokimoi*) may be made manifest." The "proven ones" of 1 Corinthians 11:19 are those who have "proved themselves" in 1 Corinthians 11:28. I don't believe that this passage requires an inward act of contemplating and evaluating one's sins. It is does not refer to an internal, subjective individual act at all. Christ's Table should be approached with demonstration of faithfulness, ecclesiastical faithfulness. Not just subjective contemplation, but objective demonstration of one's behavior with respect to the body is demanded.

The next question is what does 1 Corinthians 11:29 mean? What are we being commanded to do at the end of the passage when Paul says, "For the one who eats and drinks, eats and drinks judgment upon himself, not discerning/judging (*diakrino*) the body"? This answers the question, "How should one prove oneself?"

The answer is that one should "judge the body rightly." Again, according to the context, this most naturally means to behave in a way that takes cognizance of the whole church that is seated as one body at this meal. The point is that we dare not approach the sacramental body when we are the cause of schism and division in the corporate body! The Corinthian church came to the "common" Table in groups or parties (1 Cor. 11:21-22). The rich were over here with the best food and wine, and the poor were over there with whatever they happened to be able to bring. They were eating the Lord's Supper as a divided church!

I don't see how (in context!) this command "to discern the body" can possibly be understood as either 1) a failure to discern the location or mode of the flesh of Christ in the sacrament, or 2) a failure to reflect adequately on his death during the meal. The whole of 1 Corinthians is devoted to strife and conflict in *the body of the church*.

Paul does not say, "discern the body and blood." Whenever the sacrament is mentioned, it is mentioned as *body and blood*. Paul refers to the Communion meal as body *and* blood, eating *and* drinking, the bread *and* the cup. Verses 24-25 set out both elements. Then verse 26 says, "as often as you *eat this bread and drink this cup*." Verse 27 says, "whoever *eats the bread*

and drinks the cup of the Lord in an unworthy manner." Verse 28 says, "and so let him eat of the bread
and drink of the cup." Verse 29 says, "he who eats and
drinks, eats and drinks judgment." It is clear, then, that
if Paul were referring to discerning something about
the sacrament, he would not have written "discern the
body," but rather "discern the body and blood"! By
specifying the body only, he clearly intends to iden-
tify the sin of the Corinthian congregation—they eat
and drink at the Lord's Table as a divided *body*. The
"judging the body" is parallel to "judging ourselves" (1
Cor.11:31). One fails to "judge the body" when one
"despises the church of God" (1 Cor. 11:22).

Pay careful attention to the way Paul concludes
his exhortation in 1 Corinthians 11. Paul closes out
the chapter with a summary exhortation: "So then,
my brothers, when you come together to eat, wait for
one another. . . . so that when you meet together it may
not result in judgment" (1 Cor. 11:33, 34). Please note
that Paul does *not* summarize his warnings by reminding them to engage in rigorous, introspective self-examination before coming to the Table. He does *not*
warn them against not participating in the Supper if
they don't understand the correct interpretation of the
real presence of Jesus in the body and blood. What he
does do is tell them to "wait for each other"! Behave

like a unified community. This entire passage is about the *manner* in which the church at Corinth eats at the Lord's Supper—they partake as *a divided church*. It is not about 1) children coming to the Table, 2) intellectually challenged people coming to the Table, 3) people partaking who do not know the difference between the Reformed, Catholic, and Baptist view of the presence of Christ at the meal, or 4) people coming to the Table without adequately reflecting upon the death of Jesus. It's all about manifesting the unity of the church at the Lord's family Table.

Let me close my long answer to this question by bringing all of this to bear upon the young child Communion question. Are our children members of the body of Christ, the church? They are indeed by baptism. Why then are they cut off from *communion* with Jesus? Why do we eat as a *divided* body? Far from being a proof text against young child Communion, this passage judges traditional Presbyterianism as a church for "not discerning the body"! Why is it that when we come together as a church there are divisions among us? A great big ugly division is *manifest* at the Table between adults and children, members of the church and "half-way" members of the church. We are divided between those who are in the covenant (adults) and those who are halfway in the covenant (baptized little children).

When the family of God gathers around the Table to eat dinner with the Lord, why are the little children excluded? Do they not belong to him? Why must they be told and sometimes forcibly hindered from eating and drinking with the one with whom they are covenantally united? Have they proven themselves to be schismatic or divisive? Do *they* fail to discern the unity of the body of Christ? Are they, like the wealthy Corinthian gluttons, the *cause* of the division? If so, then by all means they should be excluded. If not, why are they denied access to Jesus' family Table? No, it is not the children who fail to discern the unity of the body of Christ; rather, we, the adult leaders of the church, are those who fail to judge the body rightly. We traditional Presbyterians have for too long "despised the church of God and humiliated those who have nothing" (1 Cor. 11:22).

The analogy with the family table is valid and powerful. All my children ate dinner with the family, even my two-year-old! They were all required to "prove themselves" before and at the table. They were all required to "judge the body" of the family. In other words, they were all required to respect the unity of the family, even the toddler in the family! If one of them failed to discern the unity of the family and started throwing food at his fifteen-year-old sister, then he was disciplined. He was learning what it means to have the privilege of eating at the table. He had to prove himself. He was required to "discern the body" before and at every meal. If he refused, he had to be disciplined.

But I have heard Presbyterian ministers say that they have "never encountered a three-year-old who is able to examine himself." But I say that one-, two-, and three-year-olds show their ability to discern the importance of the family meal in countless Christian homes every night. We begin disciplining our children at very early ages because we believe that they are capable of self-examination! Because they are members of the family, they are graciously invited to the dinner table to eat. In the context of this gracious setting, as they grow up, they gradually and with increasing maturity learn what it means to behave in accordance with the privilege of family table fellowship. They can indeed "prove themselves." They begin to learn very early what is the meaning and significance of the family meal, and they learn how to behave in accordance with that significance. Surely, one can see the application to the Lord's Table.

So who really are those who are guilty of not "discerning the Lord's body"? Are they the little baptized children of the church who have not yet attained intellectual maturity or are they those who bar such children from the Table? Who really is guilty of sinning against the "body of Christ"? Christ's little ones or traditionalist Presbyterian theologians and pastors who continue to oppose the unity of the entire body of Christ, adults and children, around his Table? If Paul's fundamental concern is the unity of the body of Christ around the Table, and if his admonitions to "prove yourself" and "discern the body" are directed at those who cause *divisions* in the ecclesiastical body of Christ, then, in my humble opinion, traditional Presbyterian theologians and pastors have some serious self-examination to perform before they come to the Lord's Table.

Questions Relating to Church History

Jesus means Savior. Jesus is the Savior. Those whom he doesn't save, having nothing to save in them, well for them he isn't Jesus. Well now, if you can tolerate the idea that Christ is not Jesus for some persons who have been baptized, then I'm not sure your faith can be recognized as according with the sound rule. Yes, they're infants, but they are his members. They're infants, but they receive his sacraments. They are infants, but they share in his Table to have life in themselves." —Augustine, Sermon 174, 7

Question 7: Is this practice novel? Is there any precedent in Church history for admitting young children to the Table? What does the history of the church teach us about this question?

Throughout the first thousand years of church history, baptized infants and small children communed with the congregation every week at the Lord's Table. This can be established by consulting any scholarly history of the church, especially those histories which concentrate on the development of the liturgy. The Western Church began to exclude children from the Lord's Table in the Middle Ages as a result of the corruption of the meaning of the sacrament. The Eastern Orthodox church has carried on the early church tradition of receiving young children and even infants to the Communion Table. Even today they still practice paedocommunion.

The doctrine of transubstantiation, which teaches that the bread and wine are actually and really transformed into the material flesh and blood of Christ by the priest, so terrified the people that they began little by little to withdraw from the Table. The priests, too, were afraid to give such awe-inspiring morsels and sips to the people for fear that they might drop or spill some of it. The introduction of this new theology of transubstantiation triggered a new kind of Communion piety that led to a superstitious scrupulosity in handling the physical elements of the Lord's Supper. Lay people withdrew from the cup because they were afraid they might spill some of Christ's blood. Children were much too rambunctious and unpredictable even to be brought near the transubstantiated elements.

By the time of the Reformation, it was common for most Christian adults to partake only once every year or two, and then they would only receive the bread, Communion in "two kinds" being forbidden to the laity. During this time it was not considered wise, practically speaking, to try to give Communion to young children; after all, they might drop a piece of Christ's body or spill a drop of Christ's blood. By excluding children from the Table, the church effectively excommunicated them.

The Reformers were horrified by the Late Medieval *ex opera operato* conception of the manner in which grace was received through the sacrament— *like the working of a machine*: you put a quarter in and out comes a Coke; likewise, you receive the bread and wine, and grace is automatically *infused* in you. The Reformers emphasized faith as a necessary prerequisite for communing. And rightly so. Yet their conception of faith, nurtured as it was in the context of the Renaissance humanist academic tradition, was an overly intellectualistic one. They were blinded to the fact that little children may have faith and yet not have attained to the *mature knowledge* and *experience* that an adult believer possesses. Some knowledge is necessary for faith, to be sure, but the *level* of knowledge required by many in the Reformation tradition is much too high. (Incidentally, many of the late medieval forerunners of the 16th century Reformers, most notably John Huss and his followers in Bohemia, worked for the restoration of child Communion. The German Reformed theologian and pastor, Wolfgang Musculus, also argued for the restoration of baptized children to the Communion Table.)

We should carefully examine the possibility that our Reformed tradition intrudes and sometimes prevents us from appreciating the overwhelming historical and biblical evidence for young child Communion. A *tradition* has developed in the Reformed and Presbyterian church whereby a child must wait until his teenage years before applying for communing membership. This *tradition* is very well argued in the Presbyterian Church of America's majority "Report of the Ad-Interim Committee to Study the Question of Paedocommunion" (Appendix T, *Minutes of the Fifteenth General Assembly*, 516ff.). But even though the authors of this report seek to defend the traditional Reformed stance that no children be admitted to the Lord's Table before "the age of discretion," they never define what they mean by the term "age of discretion," nor do they successfully argue such a qualification from the Bible. In fact, in the substance of the report they confess: "Admittedly, Reformed practice has at times *unduly delayed* the time when a child may be prepared to respond in this active way by professing his or her faith" (emphasis mine). That is precisely what I am arguing against.

Question 8: Surely since many of the Reformers and most of the Reformed tradition after the Reformation have not admitted young children to the Table, we should be extremely cautious before we do so.

There are those who would oppose paedocommunion by constructing long lists of Reformation and post-Reformation theologians who were not in favor of admitting young children. We respect these lists. It gives us genuine pause. Of course, most of us who believe that young child Communion is a biblical practice have always known that many of the men in the Reformation and Post-Reformation period of church history were not favorable to young child Communion. We think we can explain it.

First, let's remember that "Sola Scriptura," not "anti-young-child Communion," was a cry of the Reformation. Isn't it possible, given the depth and intensity of all the battles they had to fight, that the Reformers just plain missed this issue. After all, young child Communion was not even a controversy in the sixteenth, or for that matter, the seventeenth or eighteenth centuries either. Is there no more development, no more reforming, no more purifying to accomplish in the Church of Jesus Christ after the 16th century? We think there is, and we think this is one of the fundamental areas that needs to be reformed according to the Word in the modern Church.

Second, the Reformation and post-Reformation men were never really confronted with a well-argued, covenantally-grounded rationale for admitting small children to the Table. They either rejected the early church witness as evidence of a superstitious sacramental theology, or they rejected the radical left-wing "Reformers'" arguments for paedocommunion because they came loaded down with so much extra baggage. It is possible also that these men were so encumbered with a "primacy of the intellect" or philosophical outlook that they just couldn't see it. Some would say that all of these men disagree with the interpretation of 1 Corinthians 11 given in support of the young-child Communion position. I'm not sure what this means. I find myself in agreement with the exegesis that many of these men offer for 1 Corinthians 11. Nevertheless, when it comes to working out the implications, especially the bearing of 1 Corinthians 11 on the question of small child Communion, then I find myself disagreeing with them.

And, finally, after all, what good does it really do to construct a long list of men who don't agree with young child Communion? Why does this list start in the sixteenth century? I can list the theologians of the early church who practiced young child Communion, as many or more than might be listed from the sixteenth century—Augustine, Cyprian, Athanasius, Hilary, Jerome, Rufinus, Ambrose, Prosper, Leo the Great, Gregory the Great, Cyril, Basil, Gregory of Nyssa, Gregory of Nazianzus, Epiphanius, Theodore, John Chrysostom, etc. These are the men who gave us the nicely articulated doctrines of the deity of Christ, the humanity of Christ, the Trinity, predestination, etc. Since the Reformers desired to restore the "old catholic" doctrine and liturgy, especially since they were self-designated "Augustinians," why didn't they perceive the significance of young child Communion? Your answer may be, "They understood it to be an unbiblical error," but we think they just failed to understand (for whatever reason) the robust biblical and covenantal rationale for the practice.

Pastors in the post-Apostolic church often called out "holy food for the holy people of God" when they were distributing the bread and wine. The holiness of the family of God is ritually constituted by baptism and maintained by participation in the holy meal. If our children are part of Jesus' holy family by baptism, sanctified by the Spirit in Christ, then they ought to be at the Table. Unless, of course, we want to make the Table more restrictive than Paul, who insists that the oneness of the body of Christ is manifest by those who eat of the one loaf (1 Cor. 10:17)! All those who eat of the one loaf are part of the Body of Christ; those who do not are outside of the covenant and church. The early church understood this, as Augustine argues in one of his sermons:

> Those who say that infancy has nothing in it for Jesus to save, are denying that Christ is Jesus for all believing infants. Those, I repeat, who say that infancy has nothing in it for Jesus to save, are saying nothing else than that for believing infants—infants, that is, who have been baptized in Christ—Christ the Lord is not Jesus. After all, what is Jesus? Jesus means Savior. Jesus is the Savior. Those whom he doesn't save, having nothing to save in them, well, for them, he isn't Jesus. Well now, if you can tolerate the idea that Christ is not Jesus for some persons who have been baptized, then I'm not sure your faith can be recognized

as according with the sound rule. Yes, they're infants, but they are his members. They're infants, but they receive his sacraments. They are infants, but they share in his Table, in order to have life in themselves (Augustine, *The Works of Saint Augustine*, ed. John E. Rotelle, trans. Edmund Hill, 11 vols. Part 3—Sermons. [New Rochelle, New York: New City Press, 1992], 5:261).

Practical Questions

So then, my brothers, when you come together to eat, share with one another. —1 Corinithians 11:33

Question 9: What dangers are involved in waiting until children are teenagers for them to be admitted to the Table? Isn't that practice safer?

The sacrament of the Lord's Supper is meant to teach us that all life comes from God; life is a gift of God apart from our works. We passively receive life from God and in response give thanks (thus, one of the most important names for the Lord's Supper from early times has been the "Eucharist," which means "thanksgiving"). When children must wait until they have achieved some level of understanding or have undergone some stereotypical "conversion" experience, then they might easily get the idea *that one must earn the right* to come to the Table of the Lord to receive *life*. When we bar little children from coming to the Lord's Table, we are subtly but effectively communicating to them that they need to *do some kind of works* before they will be entitled to come to Jesus' family meal. Most older children that I have taught and questioned about this think that coming to the Lord's Table is an *attainment*, rather than a *gift*. This is dangerous.

As I have had an opportunity to teach in Christian schools as well as in junior and senior high Sunday school classes, I have noticed that often our own adolescents are bewildered about their place and status in the church. Are they members or not? Do the adults in the church consider them believers or not? "Just what is our status?" they ask.

Covenant children who have been baptized, have grown up in the church, have learned to sing "Jesus loves me," and have been encouraged all along (in Sunday School) to trust in Jesus and take comfort in the fact that they are God's children—these kids are doubly confused when they get in junior high and high school and the church begins to treat them, at best, as enigmas and, at worst, as *not yet converted*. This problem is compounded when "youth speakers" are paraded before them, many of which talk about how they grew up in church and they *used* to think that they were

Christians until they had a traumatic conversion experience in college.

Teenagers pick up on the implications of this kind of talk. They are tempted to think something like this:

> We thought we were Christians. Even though we have been taught that Jesus loves us, and even though we *think* that we are trusting Jesus for our salvation, well, now that we hear this man speaking, maybe we really aren't Christians *because we haven't experienced the kind of conversion that he is talking about.* And if we are not genuine Christians, nor can we be until we undergo this conversion experience, then why should we try to behave like Christians now? We'll wait until we have the experience in college. Come to think of it, are we really Christians in the eyes of the church? Do the adults of our congregation really see us as possessing full status as Christians? Well now, if we are not yet genuine Christians, then why should we try to live like Christians?

Admitting children to the Table of the Lord early on not only will remind them of God's love and his gift of life for them (regardless their intellectual or experiential capacity), but it will encourage the body of

Christ to *consider these children as Christians* and to *expect* of them *obedience* to Christ and the Christian character that is appropriate to their age and capacity.

Question 10: What about children and adults who are mentally impaired? Should they be at the Table?

Yes. Not only are our youngest children excluded, but in my experience many Reformation churches also exclude the mentally handicapped members of the covenant as well. Baptized autistic children, for example, as well as others who are mentally incapacitated are not permitted to come to the Table because they cannot complete the class work and/or successfully articulate their faith to a room full of blue-suited elders. We may not say this out loud to them, but we have ordered our Communion meals such that the meals communicate to the weak and handicapped: "You are not really a part of this body," and even, "We're not sure that you ever can be." Or what about older saints who suffer from dementia, Alzheimer's, or some other form of mental incapacitation? Should they be excluded because they can no longer articulate what does and doesn't happen when the Supper is observed? For those younger and weaker members of the body of Christ that cannot and may never be able to benefit from the highly intellectual and discursive forms of communication in our churches, barring them from the Table removes from them one of the only means of grace that they might "understand." Truly the head has said to the feet, "I have no need for you" (1 Cor. 12:21).

Question 11: If children participate in the Lord's Supper before reaching intellectual and spiritual maturity, isn't it highly likely that they will misunderstand the true nature and meaning of the sacrament by treating it as a sacred act in itself?

This is a common argument used against the practice of young child Communion: immature children who partake may develop erroneous ideas about the meaning of the sacrament. I don't find this argument very compelling. The argument could be reversed. Children who are *excluded* from the sacrament—whose little hands are constantly slapped when they reach for the bread as it is passed around—are just as likely, maybe more so, to develop unfortunate ideas about the meaning of the sacrament. If we are concerned about guarding against a sacerdotal or magical understanding of the sacrament, then we should allow our children to partake at a young age. In the context of eating, they should learn the simple yet profound truth that Jesus loves them so much that he wants to eat dinner with them. They should be taught to trust in Jesus for spiritual food at the Lord's Table, just as they trust their father and mother to feed them at the family table. Just what are we teaching our children when we exclude them from the Table? That only adults can come to Jesus? That Jesus only feeds people who have reached a certain age or a certain level of intellectual sophistication?

Behind this question lies an unwarranted assumption: that little children are naturally inclined to regard the sacraments in a Roman Catholic sense. I have never seen an *argument* for this assumption. What meaning does a small child attach to participation in Communion? That depends on what we teach them to believe about the sacrament. The children will quite "naturally" grow into an understanding of the sacrament determined by the theological framework of interpretation within which the parents and the church operate. What better way to teach our children the meaning of the sacrament than by explaining its meaning in the context of their participation. Do we wait until our children have acquired a mature understanding of prayer before we allow them to pray? No, they come to understand what prayer means in the context of praying. Of course, our children will have an incomplete, and often immature understanding of the meaning of the sacrament, but we need to properly distinguish between *incomplete* and *inaccurate* comprehension. And I can't resist asking: who really comprehends how the Lord feeds us at his Table? Most adults have an entirely appropriate child-like understanding of what the Lord gives us at his Table.

Question 12: When should my child eat and drink at the Lord's Table?

Baptism qualifies one to be at the Lord's Table. This is because baptism unites us to Christ and his body, the Church. Everyone who is baptized is a member of the body of Christ.

> For just as the body is one and has many members, and all the members of the body, though many, are one body, so it is with Christ. For in one Spirit we were all baptized into one body—Jews or Greeks, slaves or free—and all were made to drink of one Spirit. For the body does not consist of one member but of many (1 Cor. 12:12-14).

Those who eat at the Table are participants in the body of Christ:

> The cup of blessing that we bless, is it not a participation in the blood of Christ? The bread that we break, is it not a participation in the body of Christ? Because there is one bread, we who are many are one body, for we all partake of the one loaf (1 Cor. 10:16-17).

Baptism qualifies one to partake of the Lord's Table because the Lord's Table is for the *whole* body of Christ, not just some members of the body. It turns out that the Corinthian church was not actually performing the Lord's Supper, according to Paul.

> When you come together it is not for better but for worse. . . for when you come together as a church, I hear there are divisions among you. . . . When you come together it is not the Lord's Supper that you eat (1 Cor. 11:17-21).

Why does Paul accuse the Corinthians of *not* eating the Lord's Supper at their gatherings? Because they are not all eating together, but there are factions evident at the Table. The Supper is meant to embody the unity of the body of Christ. And so what a local church does in her Eucharistic liturgy is a confession of the nature of the church. If Gentiles do not eat with Jews, then the body of Christ is rent asunder (Gal. 2:11-14). If the poor are marginalized, then the church family includes the wealthy but not others (1 Cor. 11:20-22). If the weak and most unseemly are unwelcome to the Table, then are they even full members of the body of Christ (1 Cor. 12:14-26)?

> The eye cannot say to the hand, "I have no need of you," nor again the head to the feet, "I have no need of you." On the contrary, the parts of the body that seem to be weaker are indispensable, and on those parts of the body that we think less honorable we bestow the greater honor, and our unpresentable parts are treated with greater modesty, which our more presentable parts do not require. But God has so composed the body, giving greater honor to the part that lacked it, that there may be no division in the body, but that the members may have the same care for one another. If one member suffers, all suffer together; if one member is honored, all rejoice together (1 Cor. 12:21-26).

Every baptized member of the church at Corinth is "holy" in Christ and for that reason they all share a common fellowship as the body of Christ. It should be noted here that Paul's introductory salutation and prayer embrace the children of believers since they are explicitly said to be "holy" in 1 Corinthians 7:14. Later in his epistle Paul will argue that even though they may be "weaker" members of the body they are to be given more honor by other "stronger" members of the body (1 Cor. 12:22–25).

How then can a church faithfully eat the sacrament that symbolizes and seals the unity of the body of Christ while systematically excluding the weakest members of the body? Is the Table only for the strong and intelligent? Are our children not "holy"? Are not all the baptized of the church "members of the body"? (1 Cor. 12:12). If so, do we rightly "discern" or "judge" the body of Christ when we exclude certain baptized members of his body because they are smaller or weaker or less intelligent? If the meal is Holy Communion, and eating at this Table is one of the definitive ways in which God's holy people are set apart from the world, then all those that are holy ought to be included in the meal—including our children, those who are so precious to our Savior (Mark 10:14).

So when can my son or daughter participate in Communion? They have the *right* to do so because of their baptism. Practically speaking, they should partake when they are able to eat solid food. We don't believe that there's an inherent power in the elements such that force feeding babies has some sort of spiritual benefit. The Supper is a ritual meal for those who can eat and drink. This includes very small children. They can sense when they are excluded and when they are part of the community. Small children should grow up in the church never knowing a time when they did not eat and drink with Jesus at his Table. They will not have been "admitted" to the Table after being quizzed and found to be qualified. They will have experienced being loved and cared for by God from the womb. Their baptism confirmed this and their experience eating and drinking at the Table with the rest of the body of Christ will sustain their knowledge of God's love in Christ. The Psalms and other Scriptures encourage us all to think this way (Ps. 8:2; 22:9-10; 51:5; 139:13-16; Matt. 21:16; Luke 1:44).

Question 13: Should children admitted to the Table become voting members as well? If they are full communing members of the church, how can they be forbidden the right to vote?

Is there a difference between eating at the Table and actively participating in the decision-making processes in the church? In other words, can children be allowed to eat without also being allowed to vote about matters related to the life and future of the congregation? Can they eat but not vote (voting being the modern way in which members participate in the governing the congregation)?

Does the family analogy work for the church family? The argument for setting a voting age is quite simple and, I believe, compelling. It is simply that the requirements for eating, that is, receiving food from Jesus at his family Table are not the same as what is required to make mature decisions that affect the life and future of the family. It is one thing to be part of the family, but something else entirely to participate discerningly in family decision-making.

Think about what happens in any normal home. The children eat at the family table and participate in the fellowship and conversation at the meal, but they do not normally deliberate with Mom and Dad about decisions regarding family finances, legal issues, the management of the family's property, etc. The intellectual capacity and experience necessary to make those kinds of judgments, whether regarding the management of a particular household or in regard to the affairs of a particular congregation is something that generally comes with maturity. Such decision-making requires wisdom. Wisdom comes with age, knowledge, and experience.

This is not merely a maxim of common sense. The Scriptures teach this.

> He who is faithful in what is least is faithful also in much; and he who is unjust in what is least is unjust also in much (Luke 16:10).

> When I was a child, I spoke as a child, I understood as a child, I thought as a child; but when I became a man, I put away childish things (1 Cor. 13:11).

> Brethren, do not be children in understanding; however, in malice be babes, but in understanding be mature (1 Cor. 14:20).

> ... we should no longer be children, tossed to and fro and carried about with every wind of doctrine, by the trickery of men, in the cunning craftiness of deceitful plotting... (Eph. 4:14).

> For though by this time you ought to be teachers, you need someone to teach you again the first principles of the oracles of God; and you have come to need milk and not solid food. For everyone who partakes only of milk is unskilled in the word of righteousness, for he is

a babe. But solid food belongs to those who are of full age, that is, those who by reason of use have their senses exercised to discern both good and evil (Heb. 5:12-14).

If our young children do possess a knowledge of the fundamental things of the Gospel ("Jesus loves me, this I know" or "He died for my sins"), that does not mean they possess the wisdom and skill necessary to understand and judge ecclesiastical doctrine, or legal and governmental matters. Even if we restricted our "communing/voting membership" interviews to thirteen-year-olds, they would not yet have the necessary life experience and maturity to be given the privilege of voting on such matters.

Even in churches that do not establish a voting age, it works out like this anyway. Younger children, even teenagers, if they do vote (and many of them don't), will vote the way their parents have advised them. This makes sense, of course— biblical sense. Young children are supposed to submit to and obey their parents. If their parents advise them to vote a certain way or not to vote at all, they have no independent rights and privileges in relation to their parents. (I am, of course, assuming that the parents are not commanding them to do something immoral or unlawful. If they did, then the children would have recourse to the elders of the church or even the civil magistrate in some cases.) In any normal Christian household, therefore, there would be no reason for the children to vote independently of the parents.

Jesus, himself the perfect human, "grew in wisdom and stature" (Luke 2:52). When he was a boy, he sat before Israel's teachers asking questions and listening (Luke 2:46), but he did not assume the right to judge his elders or discern the errors of Israel and the proper direction it must take. That came when he was older.

Confusing these two issues (coming to the Table and voting) has led some churches to withhold Communion from young people until they are old enough to make mature decisions about matters that are often decided at congregational meetings. But this is to place an unbiblical hurdle before those coming to the Table. Where in the Bible is "knowledge" or "maturity" a prerequisite for eating and drinking?

For the record, we should not assume that "voting" is the best way to enact the biblical principle that the people should have a say in those who rule over them. Voting is something modern, and I suppose that since it is the normal way in which modern people express their convictions, it may be allowed in the church. The right to vote, however, does allow the communing member to participate in *passing judgment* when the church meets as a council.

Surely one can discern the significant differences between *eating* at the Lord's Table and *passing judgments* in the church's council. What happens in your families? Children are invited to the family table to eat, but they are not invited to participate in the family's decision-making process. Why? That duty belongs to the father and mother since they have the prerequisite wisdom and experience to make wise judgments about family finances, plans, etc.

Therefore, a church's constitution should have a two-fold distinction within the membership of the church: 1) members that do not vote (baptized children or Christians who partake of the Lord's Supper but are not old enough or mature enough to vote); and 2) communing members who are also voting members.

Question 14: Explain the benefits of young children coming to the Table.

Well, I could list all the benefits that accrue to the faithful participant at the Lord's Table, whether adult or child, but maybe it might be best to give two examples of conversations that might happen during Communion. Some can no doubt testify to the accuracy and frequency of this kind of conversation between a mother (or father) and her young son during the Lord's Supper at a traditional Presbyterian church:

> "Mommy, why can't I eat and drink with everyone?" the child asks.
>
> The parent responds, "You will have to wait until you're older, son."
>
> "Does Jesus still love me?"
>
> "Yes, of course he loves you, son."
>
> "Then why can't I eat dinner with him, Mommy?"
>
> "Because you have to wait. Now stop asking questions, I'm trying to concentrate."
>
> "But what am I supposed to do, Mommy?"
>
> "Just be quiet. . . . Here, you can draw. The service is almost over."

Or what about this conversation (one that I doubt has ever occurred but is *assumed* in most of Reformed theological discussions on this topic).

"Daddy, why can't I eat some bread?"

"You're not ready yet, son."

"What do I have to do to get ready?"

"Well, you have to be really converted. You have to be a real Christian."

"Oh, really, Dad? I thought I was a Christian? Do I have to do something else? I'm baptized."

"It's like this, son. You might think you are a Christian, but you could be wrong. Have you been born again, son? Have you been regenerated?"

"Gee, Dad, I don't know. How can I tell? When will I know when I've got what it takes to come to the Table? I believe in Jesus. Isn't that enough?"

"That's enough questions for now, son. The bread is coming down the aisle and I have to concentrate."

Here is an example of the kind of conversation that *ought* to take place during the Communion meal when the young covenant child communes with the family and the rest of the local body of Christ.

> A three-year-old boy asks his father just before Communion, "Daddy, why do we eat bread and drink wine in church? What does it mean?"

> His father responds, "Jesus loves you, son. Just like Dad and Mom love you and feed you dinner every day. Jesus loves you too and he wants you to know that you are part of his family. He wants you to trust him for everything, son."

> "Why is everybody talking, Dad?"

> "Don't you remember? This is a family meal for the church. We greet one another and acknowledge one another just like we do when we eat dinner at home with the family.

> "Is there anything else I should do, Dad?"

> "In a moment, when the food is passed, and you eat the bread and drink the wine, pray that God would remember his covenant and be gracious to you. Jesus died on the cross for you. That's how much he loves you."

"I'm so glad that I get to eat dinner with Jesus, Daddy!"

"So am I, son."

Quesion 15: What if my church does not practice paedocommunion?

If your church does not welcome young children to the Table, you will have to consider how best to address the issue with your pastor and/or elders. But if you can discuss the matter with the church leadership, be sure to behave in a gracious manner and show proper respect to those whom the Lord has placed over you. Consider Hebrews 13:17:

> Obey your leaders and submit to them, for they are keeping watch over your souls, as those who will have to give an account. Let them do this with joy and not with groaning, for that would be of no advantage to you.

Don't make this issue a divisive one in your congregation. Remember, the signature issue for the advocates of children at the Lord's Table is the unity of the whole baptized body of Christ—men, women, weak, strong, adults, and children. To create further division in the church would be counterproductive.

Moreover, submitting to your church leadership will mean that you don't try to sneak the bread and wine to your young children during communion on Sunday morning. You will have to be patient. Submit to your church's process for admittance to the Table even while you are discussing this with your pastor and elders. Conversations about matters like this can take some time. Let your children see you modeling submissive, patient behavior in your church.

Question 16: What else can I read to study this issue in more depth?

Here is a list of a few books and articles that will help if you want to study this issue in more depth. You can find many more resources at paedocommunion.com

Gallant, Tim. *Feed My Lambs: Why the Lord's Table Should Be Restored to Covenant Children*. Grande Prairie, AB: Pactum Reformanda, 2002.

Strawbridge, Gregg, ed. *The Case for Covenant Communion*. Monroe, LA: Athanasius Press, 2006. This is an excellent collection of essays by Rob

Rayburn, Peter Leithart, Tim Gallant, myself, and others.

Leithart, Peter. *Blessed are the Hungry: Meditations on the Lord's Supper*. Moscow, ID: Canon Press, 2000.

_____. *Daddy, Why Was I Excommunicated? An Examination of Leonard J. Coppes, Daddy, May I Take Communion?* Transfiguration Press, 1992.

Lee, Tommy. "The History of Paedocommunion: From the Early Church until 1500." http://tinyurl.com/3wczxx9c

Leithart, Peter. "Paedocommunion, The Gospel, and The Church." http://tinyurl.com/3bah4m4p

Robert Rayburn, "PCA Minority Report on Paedocommunion." http://tinyurl.com/mr2ztzkn

Printed in the USA
CPSIA information can be obtained
at www.ICGtesting.com
LVHW022034041124
795693LV00021B/49